THE SECRET OF THE ROTHSCHILDS

And The Doom Cycle it Could Mean for Bitcoin

Original Edition: Mary E. Hobart,
New Edition: Brian Erickson

Publisher of Original Unedited Work: Charles H. Kerr & Company Chicago, 1898

ISBN-13: 9798630335401

Cover design by: Brian Erickson
Printed in the United States of America

thou shalt lend unto many nations, but thou shalt not borrow — Moses, Deut 15:6

This century will not close before we shall have a general re-organization of international relations throughout the world and alliances and combinations on new lines to meet conditions which have long been changing silently and slowly and have now reached the stage where the bud must burst into flower. —Memoranda of Baron Rothschild to Lord Salisbury, 1896.

CONTENTS

PREFACE TO THE 2020 VERSION

This is an interesting work, both to me personally, and as an artifact of history.

Isn't it interesting that there have been whistleblowers on the Rothschilds for over a hundred years? Probably even longer if a person stumbled upon the right archive.

I think any reader can learn a lot from this book, whether it's your first time learning about Fractional Reserve Banking and this banking family, or whether you've never seen this account before of damage done to U.S.A. and economies around the world, for that matter.

I can't stress enough to consider this book's subtitle: And the Doom Cycle it Could Mean for Bitcoin, as you read through this and get to the concept of "the island," which has finite money on it. I think every Crypto Currency I've ever seen is finite, so, as you'll see here, Crypto debt would be far worse than currency debt. I lay all this out in my Editor's Notes, so don't skip those if you want to understand why the book has that subtitle.

In terms of editing, I broke this into more sections after the chapters and named them, whereas before they were only numbered. I also updated a bit of the language, cleaned up the chart to a less confusing format, and made general grammatical corrections along with my thoughts laid out in 'Editor's Notes.'

This came from a pamphlet, and the author seems quite knowledgeable, but there were basic errors that a good proofreading would've sorted out.

Lastly, it is old, and being the age that it is, some things look very outdated, such as talk of the Gold Standard. Not many people alive today remember moving off the Gold Standard, certainly

not the majority. However, the principles are sound, and the economics of it changes no more than mathematics does due to the passage of time.

I had fun reading and editing this, and I hope it enlightens many a reader, who don't understand why money is so hard to grow.

Thank you.

PREFACE TO THE ORIGINAL TEXT

It has been impossible within the narrow limits of this work to enter into an exhaustive discussion of all the phases, principles and complex relations of the "money question." Neither has it been possible to treat even in a limited manner of the "seven great conspiracies" which have been enacted into law by venal legislators and which have greatly intensified in number and magnitude the financial disasters which naturally arise under our present system of money, even when honestly administered. But that which has been attempted is to establish, beyond disputation, by analysis and comparative demonstration the fallacious principles upon which our money system is founded and without a knowledge of which it is impossible to understand the complex and confused conditions which now pervade all departments of our social fabric. The reader is admonished that there is no royal road which leads to the understanding of the science of government any more than there is to the understanding of geometry or astronomy.

If a practical comprehension of this subject is ever acquired it must be through the patient study and careful investigation of the relations which exist between all our varied business transactions.

The teacher who told his pupil that the best way to state a problem in compound proportion was to "guess at it" illustrates the teaching of political economy as it has been and is still taught. The economists, like the teacher, have never studied deep enough to discover that this science is not governed by the laws of "chance" but by principles which are as fixed and unchangeable as those by principles govern any branch of mathematics. The confusion and turmoil now agitating the world come because

our teachers have been "guessing at it." They have been dealing in rhetoric when they should have been delving in numbers and philosophy. Rhetoric may, indeed, brighten and beautify economic discussion when once the principles have been established, but till then we must content ourselves with the soberest prose.

If the laboring people of America ever succeed in bettering their conditions it will only be after they themselves have mastered the principles of the systems through which their oppressors plunder them.

It is not true that "what a man does not know does not, hurt him." He is hurt just the same, knowledge or no knowledge. But when he does not know what hurts him he is powerless in his defense. All the sufferings and wrongs of the laboring people are endured because they do not understand the methods used by the so-called "better classes" to filch from them the rewards of their toil. The betterment of their conditions can only be accomplished through the betterment of their knowledge. With this view the author places before the public this unpretentious effort, regretting that space does not permit a more complete examination of the subject discussed. Many phases of the money, question which are of vital importance have necessarily been omitted. The work is designed to be in every sense elemental—an aid to those who have been unable through the complex discussions to gather a clear understanding of this vastly important subject. If this object shall be accomplished the author will be richly rewarded for the thought expended upon it. After carefully reading this book the reader is kindly requested to pass or mail it to some other person, with the request that he in like manner shall pass it on, in order that these truths may be more effectually disseminated among all classes.

Mary E. Hobart.

New Whatcom, Wash.

CHAPTER I.

A Problem for Scientists to Solve.

I see in the near future a crisis arising, which unnerves me and makes me tremble for the safety of my country. As a result of the war corporations have been enthroned, and an era of corruption in high places will follow, and the money power will endeavor to prolong its reign, by working on the prejudices of the people, until all wealth is aggregated in the hands of the few, and the Republic is lost. —Abraham Lincoln, 1866.

By some machination, by some incantation, honest or otherwise, thirty thousand people have become possessed of thirty-five billions, or half the wealth of this great nation. Mr. Speaker, this is the most appalling statement that ever fell upon mortal ears. — John J. Ingalls, United States Senate, 1890.

The people of the United States are now thirty-two billion dollars in debt. —Speech of Jos. M. Walker, M.C., House of Representatives, 1882.

Organize under whatsoever form of government man may, under a Republic or a Principality, under a Kingdom or an Empire, there seems to be some secret law which continually concentrates the wealth which the many make into the hands of the idle few. Happy our generation if science sometime gives the key. —Blanqui's History of Political Economy.

These quotations furnish data from which no thoughtful student of public affairs can or will turn with indifference. Indeed, the striking character of each is sufficiently important to arrest the attention of the dullest dullard belonging to that species of the genus homo known as the American voter. The first, a prophecy from one of the wisest and purest of statesmen, predicating conditions then existing which if not arrested would overwhelm the young Republic and dethrone popular government. The second declares that the half-way station of this remarkable prophecy has already been passed. The third announces conditions which unerringly point to the final consummation of Abraham Lincoln's prophetic vision. The last asserts that this is the trend of human affairs under whatsoever form of government, man has thus far organized; that these unjust relations are the result of some secret and unknown law, which science has not yet unlocked; that happiness, the goal of all human endeavor, will be the inheritance of all men, when an intelligent solution of this problem has been attained. The importance of this last fact is sufficient to spur the student on, in an earnest effort to discover this hitherto undiscovered law.

In our search we shall rigidly deduce from known facts logical, philosophical and mathematical conclusions, for by no methods less than these can we reach a scientific solution. Statistics are the most reliable and best authenticated facts that we have from which to deduce logical conclusions.

In 1865 the Secretary of the United States Treasury, Hugh McCulloch, in his annual report, made this remarkable statement: "The people are out of debt and consequently prosperous." By a comparison of the statistics of the financial failures of that year with the two previous years—1863-4—and the following year—1866 —with the failures of the five years previous to 1863 and of those which have followed 1866 we can readily give credence to the

Secretary's report, that to an extent greater than had ever before existed the people of this country were out of debt.

By these statistics, we find that for the years of 1863, 1864, 1865, 1866, the business failures were respectively 485, 502, 530, 532, while from the year 1857 to 1862 the failures ranged from 4,932 to 6,993, and from 1866 to 1896 they have ranged from 2,386 to over 15,000. Now when we remember that the financial failures taken for a series of years must be the index to a very truthful degree of the debts of the people, we must admit the fact that these years were years when the people were comparatively out of debt, and when out of debt prosperous.

At this time, let it be remembered, the American people had existed upon this continent as a nation over two hundred years, and as an independent government nearly a hundred years, yet at the close of a gigantic internecine war the Secretary of the Treasury — a high official of the United States, sworn to tell the truth — says the people are out of debt, and these statistics unquestionably prove that his statement was correct.

Twelve years from this date (1877) a United States Senator—Hon. Daniel Voorhees—who had an enviable reputation as a financier of unquestioned ability, stated on the floor of the Senate chamber that the people of the United States were from six to ten billion dollars in debt, and unless silver should be remonetized that debt could never be paid. Fifteen years later Hon. Jos. M. Walker, member of Congress from Massachusetts, stated in a speech delivered March, 1892, that the people were thirty-two billion dollars in debt.

Five years later, and reliable statisticians estimate that our debts have attained the gigantic proportions of forty billion dollars, aggregating a sum of more than five times all the metallic money of the world, an inconceivable and incomprehensible number. How incomprehensible this amount is we may partially understand when we find by computation that it would require forty persons, beginning at the age of twenty years and counting forty thousand each day, except Sundays and holidays, to live each to the age of one hundred and four years before the task of counting would be completed. How many years of unremitting toil will be required of our boys and girls to pay this monstrous debt the future alone can tell.

These statistical statements reveal a GROWTH OF DEBT which constitutes our problem. The solution of this problem is of universal significance to all the American people, regardless of politics, creed, color or condition. The prosperity of all men is affected by this gigantic debt, because the ever-increasing interest upon it enters into and augments the price of every article of consumption. It is a consuming fire, a living demon, a raging beast going up and down the highways of the nation devouring the substance of the people. It is a dark cloud of ruin overshadowing three-fourths of all the homes in the land. This problem of debt is no new problem. It is the problem of the ages. Again and again, during the history of mankind, have cities, states and kingdoms been brought face to face with this demon of evil, this devourer of men, this destruction of empires, this death of civilization. The highways of six thousand years are strewn with the wrecks of men and nations who have bowed in meek submission to its arbitrament. In its devastating march it spares neither Greek nor Jew; neither pagan nor Christian; neither Republic nor Empire. Philosophers, poets, seers and prophets have bewailed the desolation that has marked its pathway, in the language of sublime sympathy and patriotic devotion. With marvelous power and pathos, they have portrayed the effects and conditions that have followed in the trail of this unknown and undescribed highwayman, but not even the immortal genius of a Bacon, a Milton, a Newton, nor a Mill seems to have taken any comprehensive recognition of the Titanic power of evil over the fortunes and happiness of men encompassed in, and arising from conditions produced by debt.

The necessity for the analysis of causes, which produce, enlarge, and continue it, appears to have escaped their attention. But in the general uplift of humanity all secrets shall be revealed; all phenomena shall be explained; all problems shall find solutions. As every event in life has a relation to all other events, and may be traced—if we possess sufficient data—so every problem arising from human activity has a rational and logical solution.

Editor's Note:

> *My commentary on this, is that even though this is clearly long ago, it amazes me that the debt the author is talking about sounds almost identical to our debt today.*

> *Sure, it's done a bit differently with the way countries loan to each other, but a loan is a loan, and it works the same way. What they do nowadays is add in factors like currency devaluation, the big central banks and their games, so on top of everything to come in the pages ahead that lays out what debt is exactly, money can become worthless in a way the author may not have been able to imagine, because in her day, money was at least worth something, because it was based on gold. Now, our money is sort of based on oil, and it's also based on printing it, or not, and controlling the supply. So, everything is royally messed up now, royally.*

CHAPTER II

RESTATEMENT AND SOLU-TION OF PROBLEM

Given seventy million people occupying the best part of the best continent on the globe, valued at sixty-two billion dollars; on which valuation, after a period of thirty years of intense activity, in labor skilled and unskilled, exercised in the development of farms, mines and factories, in the building of cities, villages, towns, and railroads, in commerce, inventions, and speculation, said seventy million people find themselves at this date (1898) owing somebody or many somebodies over forty billion dollars.

To give a logical and philosophical cause for these disastrous conditions will be the effort of this pamphlet. The whole truth concerning this matter must be scientifically ventilated. No misleading falsehood nor seductive sophistry can alleviate the misery now so prevalent throughout the land caused by this gigantic debt. The constitution and make-up of our social organization must be analyzed, its laws of action formulated, the relations of these laws traced and the rights of individuals in their social organization clearly established.

It may be observed that this debt of forty billion is owed in dollars. Nothing but dollars, and yellow metallic dollars at that, will be received in payment or liquidation of this debt. Hence the yellow metallic dollar becomes one of the main factors in the solution of this problem. As the metallic dollar is a definite thing, which can be estimated and measured, it is therefore a mathematical quantity, and all operations with it are mathematical operations. A failure to record these operations will in no way affect the results which mathematically follow. If we can formulate these operations we can solve our problem.

What is the dollar, what is its function and from what condition of society arises the necessity for its use?

The dollar is a specified number of grains of gold or silver, on which the government has placed its official stamp, stating that it is a dollar, and shall be received by all creditors in payment of a dollar's debt. Its function is two-fold, for it acts in the hands of the holder both as a receipt and check. A receipt for a dollar's worth of production or service, which the holder has parted with for the benefit of society or some member thereof. It is also a check entitling the holder to draw upon society for one dollar's worth of production or service, which society or some member thereof may desire to part with. The material on which this stamp is placed cannot affect its power, or function. The social necessity which calls for its use was philosophically answered by a school boy of twelve, who said we need it to buy things with, because we don't know how to make all the things we need. In more scientific language civilized man has entered a social condition, which may be designated a division of labor, which defined means that condition of society in which some men raise wheat, some corn, some cotton, some rice, some produce or manufacture sugar, some flour, some leather, some make bread, some shoes, some hats, some coats, etc., etc.

This social condition makes every member of society interdependent; each works for all and all work for each. Every man produces a surplus of some commodity, or renders some service which he must dispose of, in order to procure those commodities and services which he cannot produce or render.

Equity and the eternal law of righteousness (right action) demands that every man be protected in the disposal of his commodities, also in the purchase of other commodities, so that he receive equal for equal and equivalent for equivalent.

Nothing short of this can fulfill the will of the Father on earth as it is in Heaven. Neither will this great question ever be settled until settled upon this basis. A division of labor once endorsed and entered into by a nation of people bestows upon that people the right to make provision for the exercise of three powers, namely, the power of communication, the power to transfer goods from place to place or transportation, and the power to transfer the ownership of goods from person to person (or the power of exchange). These three powers inhere in the constitution and social make-up of society, and are the prerogatives and functions belonging to the whole people.

Every citizen has the right to an equal and inalienable ownership in these powers, and he has the right to demand of the collectivity (government) that these powers be furnished him in sufficiency to meet all the necessities of his condition at cost. Otherwise if these truly governmental functions be delegated to individuals they may be so manipulated, monopolized, cornered and controlled that wholesale robbery, exploitation and slavery will be the final result. No reasonable denial can be given to these self-evident propositions. There is no reasonable or logical basis for the assumption that any man or corporation of men should receive tribute from society or any member thereof for the use of any one of these powers above the actual cost. The men who raise wheat, and desire to trade with the men who raise cotton, have an inalienable right, by reason of their social condition (division of labor), to demand protection in the exercise of the three powers of communication, transportation and exchange, without paying more than the actual cost of these utilities, and if any man receive more than this, he is living from another man's exertion without giving an equivalent, and society has incorporated an element of inequality, which has the power, in time, to absorb all wealth into the hands of the operators of these truly governmental but usurped powers. Hence it becomes the solemn duty of society to establish, own and operate these three powers of franchise AT COST to the whole people. Successful denial of these fundamental propositions cannot be made.

We are now ready to examine in what way the United States government, which is supposed to be "of the people, for the people and by the people," has provided for these three powers, and inquire how its citizens are protected in the exercise of these inalienable and imprescriptable rights and immunities. The power of communication is secured by the establishment of postoffices, telegraphs and telephones. The first is under the supervision of the general government, and its service is rendered to all in sufficiency, at cost, being, the best-managed business in the United States. Telegraphs and telephones are supplied by private corporations, for which service the people who use them pay the cost of operation and besides a bonus of millions to capitalists whose privileges and franchises are given to them by law, and their exploitations sanctioned by the Federal courts.

The power to transfer goods from place to place is secured mostly by railroads, steamboats, and ships. These, too, are owned by private individuals and corporations, and are operated on the splendid business principle of charging all the traffic will bear and sometimes something more. This is the worst managed business in the United States, where more strikes and labor difficulties occur than along any other line. Neither, although exacting enormous tariffs, are they able to pay their debts, but yearly thousands of miles pass into the hands of receivers under the Federal courts. We are now prepared to examine the methods by which we obtain the power of exchange, or the power to transfer the ownership of goods from person to person, which when we have done will reveal a debt-refunding system which has created the debt we owe ($40,000,000,000) and the concentration of thirty-five billion dollars of wealth into the possession of thirty thousand people, or one-twentieth of 1 percent of the population.

For a period of time so long past that history gives no hint whence the origin of the thought, men have been taught to believe that governments had no power, and could devise no methods by which individuals could be protected in the exchange of their production, except as one commodity was exchanged for another of equal value; that security and safety in transferring goods from person to person rests alone on the principle of taking some commodity as gold and silver and legalizing it as a measure of value and a medium by which all other commodities must be measured and exchanged.

The fallacy of such an idea may be seen when we analyze the action of law in its power to protect the commodity gold.

A owns a gold mine and works out 51,600 grains of gold, which coins an even $200. This gold is a commodity, and a product of labor. In itself it satisfies no essential or primary want of man. It cannot feed, warm, clothe or shelter him. Neither from it can any tool be made that can aid him in procuring these essentials. So much for gold and the labor expended in procuring it. B has a field, which he plows and cultivates and produces 12,000 pounds of wheat, which measures 200 bushels. B's labor has been useful in producing a commodity which satisfies the most essential want of man. Both wheat and gold are commodities and must be so classified. Society in its stupidity declares by its legislative action that it can by law protect the gold owner in parting with his commodity gold by a piece of paper (bonds, notes and mortgages) which holds the borrower responsible for the return to A of the gold or its equivalent, at "the same time refusing to protect B in parting with his commodity wheat for the benefit of society. C desires the wheat, but before the trade can be effected he must borrow A's commodity gold, and give him a paper security that he will return it or its equivalent. This paper has no intrinsic value, yet the law behind it makes A safe in parting with his gold. The question arises why may not a piece of paper be made, so legalized that B may be secured in parting with his wheat, that he, too, will be able to receive an equivalent in return? By what logic is this discrimination drawn? Law stamped upon paper protects commodity gold; why can it not protect commodity wheat?

The second error of such a proposition may be seen in the fact that no one commodity is of sufficient magnitude to measure the value of all other commodities, and no one commodity is held in common ownership, but in a division of labor all persons in the association will need a sufficient quantity of this commodity, whatever it may be, to measure the value of and exchange all the commodities which they are capable of making and desire to exchange. Then it will be seen that the demand for money is equal to the demand for all other things. And as no commodity is equal to such an extension, commodity exchange, or the exchange of one article for another of equal value, will always prove a miserable failure. From its use a great degree of injustice will arise, because no commodity is in the hands of all persons in the nation, and some will be forced to borrow the exchange commodity (gold and silver) and submit to the terms of the loaner, which past experience has proven will be too often extortionate and usurious, or, more correctly, some individuals will be forced to pay tribute to other individuals for the privilege of making their exchanges —a principle which has been proven to be false, to justice and the structure of society. Again, as no commodity is of sufficient capacity to measure and exchange all other commodities, the necessities growing out of the division of labor will at times become so severely urgent that some men will be forced to trade with promissory notes ("credit or confidence"), which in time must be redeemed in cash or coin. If there is not a sufficient quantity of money to trade on a cash basis, there will not be sufficient to cancel debts so made; and the impossibility of redemption destroys equity and creates losses, failures, foreclosures, concentration of wealth and a debt refunding system.

In order to discover the factors or elements which have produced our debt growth of forty billion dollars it will be necessary to formulate a problem of such small dimensions as can be easily grasped and retained in the mind, but in exact conformity to the methods employed by nations using commodity exchange (gold and silver), remembering that what is true mathematically of small quantities will be true when applied to larger ones.

We will now suppose that in some far away sea is an isolated island, on which a hundred men and women have been wrecked, with no possible hope of future escape. Complaints are useless. Action is imperative. With hope and energy they assemble in convention and formulate plans for organization and the structure of a government. They are all workers and know how to do something. They therefore construct their government on the basis of a division of labor, and proceed to divide the island, giving to each an equal portion. They provide for postal and transportation service, and adopt gold as the measure of all values and a legal tender for all debts and the medium by which all commodities must be exchanged. For this action they can give no intelligent reason. On being questioned about it their only reply was we want "an honest dollar." We must have a "sound currency." On the island there proved to be but one small spot where this metal could be found, and this falls into the possession of one whom we will call A. He discovers the metal and works the mine. He succeeds in taking out 51,600 grains of gold — a cube less than two inches square — which the government coins for him into $200 free of cost and permits him to loan them to the community at ten per cent interest or increase. This is a legally constituted arrangement for securing a power of exchange, necessitated by the action of these islanders in endorsing and entering into a division of labor. Without mastering the philosophy of the effect of these legal arrangements, they have unwittingly made this man the arbiter of their fortunes. They have placed in his hands the power to forge a chain of circumstances, which will in the end give him the power to lawfully obtain possession of their productions and their homes without giving them back an equivalent. By law they have made this man the legal owner of that material (gold), which they must have or cease to live by co-operation, and return to a state of barbarism. By this ownership they have crowned him with greater power than is conferred upon kings and emperors. He is absolute monarch and dictator of every financial condition on the island. By this ownership he has the right to loan, or to refuse to loan; the right to disburse, or to hoard; and as he does the one or the other, artificial prosperity springs up, only to be withered by artificial death and depression. When he loans business flourishes; when he refuses, business languishes and dies. By these manipulations he is able to reduce prices and lower wages; to cover both gold and productions, thereby exploiting both producer and consumer. And as all roads lead to Rome so all industries yield their profits to swell his income and increase his wealth. The community is now divided into two classes—borrowers and loaner; laborers and capitalist. On the one side are the laborers with their lands equally divided, on the other side the capitalist with his two-inch cube of gold, possessing in its legal action a power to absorb wealth more rapidly than the ninety-nine laborers can create it from all their lands. The financial and material condition of these islanders may be thus diagrammed.

It will be perceived that by the two factors—land and labor—all wealth is created, and by the factor gold all wealth is measured and exchanged. Gold is not wealth nor the creator of wealth; but simply the tool by which the value of wealth is estimated and exchanged. The free and ready exchange of commodities greatly enhances the powers of production, and promotes prosperity. These advantages are ascribed to the power of gold, whereas it inheres in the easy and rapid exchange of productions, no matter by what methods this exchange is effected. We will now proceed to set in motion this financial mechanism of gold, which carries within itself the power to propagate nine-tenths of all the evil which besets the path of human endeavor. The following chart illustrates the debt-making and wealth-concentrating power of gold as it is now used in our legalized monetary system. The reader is earnestly requested to give careful attention to every detail, that he may know for himself that all which has been affirmed is susceptible of proof. A represents the banker owning a small piece of metal called gold; B. C, D, F, etc., are the laborers owning their lands from which all wealth is derived. This chart will follow the movements of these two hundred gold dollars as they circulate in society and record the various transactions which will transfer the ownership of the homes and lands of the toilers into the hands of the gold owner or capitalist. For the benefit of those who believe that whisky is the cause of all the poverty, we will assume that these islanders are all sober men, and that no intoxicant is manufactured or imported on the island.

CHART OF TRANSACTIONS

Now Called: Fractional Reserve Banking

Let A be the island's banker with a loaning capital of $200 (The island's initial sum of money)

Two Loans Created In The Year 1880:

B borrows Jan. 1st, 1880, $100 for 1 year at 10%—$110

C borrows Jan. 1st, 1880, $100 for 2 years at 10%—$120

Loan #1 Ends In 1881 And Is Re-Loaned:

D borrows Jan. 1st, 1881, $110 for 2 years at 10%—$132

Loan #2 Ends In 1882 And Is Re-Loaned:

E borrows Jan. 1st, 1882, $120 for 1 year at 10%—$132

Both Loans End In 1884:

Due the banker Jan. 1st, 1884—$264

Concurrent Loaning That Also Started In 1880 When Loans From "A" Enter The Economy

Jan. 1st, 1880, G loans F for three years $100 at 10%—$130

Jan. 1st, 1880, H sells J a horse for $100 on three years' timecent—$130

Total Of All Loans Due Debts Due Jan. 1St, 1884—$524

Money on the island to meet it—$200

Increment of unpaid debt, or DEBT GROWTH, arising in three years—$324

Editor's Note:

> *This table, while effective, may not have been written properly, or as intended by the author. It's also possible that the author, while understanding the concept of Fractional Reserve Banking, simply failed to explain it properly, because it appears, at one point, as through another $200 materialized from thin air in 1880 when G begins loaning to F. But this is explained below. It's the money entering the economy and distributing as loans.*

Let me take a brief second to explain how bank's do it, since it is a banking system. It's easier to bear in mind that bank's receive deposits and loan most of it out, with only 2-3% behind to cover withdrawals. Let's say you deposit $1,000 in Bank A, and the the bank leaves $30 in its vault and loans the rest at 10% for 1 year. So, $970 gets loaned, and, upon payment, is worth $1,067. It's important to note that this is a circle of money getting moved around, so money is flowing in and out all the time. The bank doesn't really only have $30 available for you to withdraw. Your $970 goes to Bank B which in turn keeps $29.10 as a reserve and loans $940.90 again at 10% making it now worth $1,034.99. Assuming, in a perfect world, all loans are repaid; the interest on these two loans has made the initial 1,000 worth $1,191.09, with just two banks. But, in the real world, they spread this basic concept out over multiple banks with loan after loan, and little bits held in reserve.

You have to remember that under our current Federal Reserve system, nothing backs our money. It's not gold based. If anything, it's oil based. So, they just keep printing and loaning it out. For Americans, the cash in your wallet is on loan from the Federal Reserve. If you've borrowed it, that means—yes, you pay for it. In reality, it's worth nothing except the perception that it is, which seems to be enough.

Before tracing these transactions, in order to avoid confusion, we will assume that no more dollars are coined or imported on the island, and also that the income of Banker A's farm is sufficient to meet all his expenses. We will also assume that these islanders are in possession of all needed tools and implements, such as plows, harrows, axes, hues, etc., so that they can begin the development of their farms and the production of wealth. Since these productions are of various kinds, each man desires to exchange with his neighbor. It may be observed that no exchange is possible until wealth of some form has been created, but when wealth has been produced, because of natural barriers and their legal arrangements they cannot make exchanges without asking Banker A for a loan of that commodity (gold) which by their law estimates values, exchanges wealth, and which is the only commodity crowned with the power of being a legal tender for debt. Virtually this is asking his permission for the right to trade! Stalwart laborers, from the highest profession to the lowest ditch-digger, you may create wealth by the million, but you cannot, shall not, exchange with each other until you have obtained permission of that man upon whom your laws have bestowed the right to own your power or medium of exchange.

By referring to the Chart of Transactions (COT) the reader will observe that B is the first member of society on the island whose necessities compel him to trade. Severe floods have destroyed his wheat, and he must have some for seeding. He learns that neighbor G has an abundance. To him he goes with various propositions of barter for horses, hogs and corn. G responds: None of these things do I want, friend B. I must sell for money. My taxes are even now overdue. This forces B, if he obtains the wheat, to borrow $100 of Banker A, said loan being made for one year at ten per cent. This transaction has not arisen because of B's idleness or imprudence nor from the fact that he has nothing to sell, but from his necessity and the legalized arrangements of the community in which he lives. These have forced him to give the banker $10 for the privilege of tradind—a privilege which under a system of justice would be free to all. Analyzed, this is a very peculiar transaction, having many phases. B sees no impossibility in the contract. He thinks, if he thinks at all, with the entire community, that raising wheat produces the same effect in increasing the number of dollars as mining and coining gold, that if he produces a good crop he has made money. In fact, he and all the community in which he lives believe that all that is necessary is to work hard, be sober and prudent and wealth and prosperity will follow. They do not comprehend that money cannot be increased by the production of commodities, neither by circulation.

C is another member of society who has lost his horse, and as spring approaches the same necessity which forced B forces him also. He has heard of B's transaction at the bank and follows his example. There is no way to escape, and he borrows of A the other $100 for two years, at the same rate of interest. It is pertinent to pause here and inquire of the reader if he considers these men to blame for being in debt. Have not the arrangements made by the community for securing the power or medium of exchange forced these men, through no fault of theirs, to contract these debts? Has not a debt system been established by law? And if the community co-operate on the basis of a division of labor can the people as a whole ever be free from debt, if money circulates at all? Under such a system, when all debts are paid or canceled, there will be no money in circulation and money by this system can only be put in circulation by debt. We have been thus minute in analyzing the situation surrounding these islanders because so many persons believe that a condition of debt is the fault of individuals, whereas it is plainly the fault of the arrangements which governments legalize for securing a power of exchange. This difficulty must always exist so long as any commodity is used for a medium of exchange. Closing this analysis, we will now follow these $200 as they circulate through the community, for only as we follow and record every transaction made with these dollars can we know with certainty what effect will be produced. In following the circulation of these two hundred dollars, we shall discover that their number is never increased by that circulation.

The $100 borrowed from A by B when paid to G for wheat remains $100. When G pays them out for taxes their number will still be one hundred. The same is true of the $100 borrowed by C. Wheresoever these $200 may go their original number will never increase. Plant them or trade them, sow them or reap them, scatter them or gather them, pay them out, or receive them in, deposit them in bank or stocking, their number will remain the same. To believe otherwise is to believe that which is false, and to act upon that belief is to lay the foundation for financial disaster, ruin, and national disruption. Let it be emphasized here that the number of dollars in circulation can only be increased by taking the metal and coining them or importing them from some other country. There rests a confusion in the minds of the people concerning the terms "make money" and "coin money." Governments make or coin money; the people earn it after it is coined or made. Money must be coined before it can be earned. This thought ought to be well digested. Yet startling as it may appear, B and C have never given one moment of serious thought to the subject and are entirely oblivious of the true philosophy of the situation, believing that their ability to pay debts depends entirely upon industry and prudence, whereas this ability is found in the increase of coinage, which A controls. The reader is kindly requested to note another fact. B and C, who are the two weakest members of society, by reason of their losses, are forced to pay a tax or tribute to Banker A for the use of these $200, while all the other islanders are able to secure the power of exchange free of cost, which is in itself an unjust discrimination between classes. For, when borrowed, money passes out of the hands of the borrower, it then becomes a free instrument of exchange. At the end of the year we will assume that B has been successful and raised a good crop of wheat which he is able to sell, and obtain (not make or coin) $110 which enables him to cancel his obligation with A. This transaction gives the appearance of the possibility of paying interest; refer to the COT. But let us see. Upon what did B's ability to secure this extra ten dollars depend on the assumed proposition that no more dollars have been coined? Evidently they are a part of the $100 borrowed by C and if neither he nor any other had borrowed, B's wheat could only have sold for $100 and the ten dollars of interest owed to A could not have been canceled, and the impossibility of paving interest without an increase of coinage would have appeared at once. No records having been kept, the error escapes detection. An examination of these islanders' financial condition after B pays the banker $110 will disclose the fact that society has in its possession but $90. Accustomed to having $200, the withdrawal of $110 will produce a stringency so severe that someone, who we will call D, will be forced to borrow. By chance (everything in the system is done by chance) he borrows from Banker A this same $110 and business runs fairly well again. By referring to the chart (that describes the lending process) the reader will observe that at the beginning of that year, when these islanders first created a debt, this debt was but $200, but at the beginning of the second year it had increased $20, for now C owes $110 and D' has borrowed $110. Mark this GROWTH OF DEBT. It may also be observed that the ten dollars of interest which appeared to have been paid is now refunded into another debt on D's farm.

At the close of another year we will suppose that C, whose note now falls due, has been successful in producing something for which he obtains $120, with which he pays Banker A (refer to COT). By what fact was C able to obtain $120? From the fact that D had borrowed $110 and from no other. As before, if all the members of society will count all the dollars in their possession after C has paid A, they will find the sum to be but $80. Another money famine will be produced and one who we will call E is forced to borrow. He presents his case to Banker A, who loans him the same $120 that C had paid his debt with. Again it will be apparent to the reader that this $20 supposed to have been paid by C is refunded into another debt on E's farm, and the close of the second year finds these islanders $241 in debt. The debt growth of two years has been $41 by the transactions, which have taken place at the bank alone. Other debts made by individuals outside the bank which produce debt growth will be examined later on.

By reference to the COT, the reader will see that at the end of one year D borrowed for two years and at the end of two years E borrowed for one. Consequently these two notes fall due on the same day. This is merely an accidental circumstance of no importance worth looking after, so the banker would have them believe. (What other inference can be drawn when they tell the farmers to go home and attend to their farms and let the great financiers run the money affairs of the country?) By reference to the chart it will be seen that D owes the banker $132 and E owes him the same amount. There now appears a debt of $264, which is $64 greater than the number of dollars on the island. This $64 is the debt growth of three years on the four loans of B, C, D and E, and will be found to be the sum of all the interest which has accrued upon their loans — viz., $10 upon B's note, plus $20 on C's, plus $22 on D's, plus $12 on E's. Not one dollar of interest, in reality, has been paid; has, in fact, only been re-funded into other debts on other securities. The impossibility of paying interest without an equivalent increase of money now appears, and one or both of these men must fail. Both may, add certainly will, if by chance some one has left the island for a foreign tour taking with him a hundred dollars or more, or if the original $200 was composed of $100 of gold and $100 of silver and the government in the meantime had demonetized silver, thus leaving the $100 of gold as the only debt-paying power on the island.

The point which this demonstration settles here, and settles forever, is that an increase of debt has arisen from loaning money at an interest which can only be paid by coining $64, or importing $64, or by the banker spending $64, or when the sum of these three items shall equal $64. It settles another point also, that the interest accruing on the loans in a nation must be known and also the increase of money for its extinguishment, or business will be done by methods of chance where failures and foreclosures are the inevitable results. Not one penny of interest can be paid by any other means, if the banker demands his interest in money (and whoever heard of his demanding anything else?).

By not reloaning and not recirculating the $200, can this debt of $64 of interest be paid? And what is true of this $200, is just as true of any conceivable sum and its interest.

A failure to keep the record will in no way affect the result.

The reader is requested to fix this principle firmly in his mind for future use, as we are now establishing principles for application later on in the work.

This demonstration will force the gold-standard theorist to acknowledge that unless $64 has been coined, imported or expended by the money loaners, neither of which was assumed in the hypothesis, one or both of these men must fail and be foreclosed. It will also force them to acknowledge that these islanders are doing business by methods which will produce failures and foreclosures through the impossibilities that arise unless an exact record of all debt contracts on the island is kept and a record of all moneys coined, of all moneys imported from and exported to foreign countries, of all moneys lost and taken from circulation and of all money expended by the money loaners, in order that the differences which arise between the debt contracts and the moneys provided for their extinguishment or liquidation may be known and these differences provided for. Otherwise these men are doing business by slipshod methods where panics, failures and foreclosures, with all their attendant evils of loss and concentration of wealth, depression, stagnation and want will be the inevitable result. If these islanders had kept an exact record of all their debt contracts and the times when they fell due, and by any method added $64 to their circulation, these men D and E might have escaped. Failing to keep these records and supply money to meet the debt growth one or both must fail; or they must re-fund their debts, which only defers the evil day; for by no process of re-loaning or re-circulation of these dollars, neither by greater industry nor economy, can this debt of $64 be canceled. The banker understands this and knows his power. He demands settlement, and, as this is impossible, the sheriff is ordered to foreclose at once.

Here let the reader pause and ponder. Let him measure the full magnitude of the cruel injustice imbedded in these transactions. D borrowed on a farm worth $500 and by two years' hard labor in ditching, fencing, digging out stumps, setting out fruit trees, building and repairing he has added $500 more to the value of his farm. E borrowed on a farm worth $600 and by the year's work has added $400 value to his, so that now the two farms are worth $2,000, which the money loaner is permitted to take possession of, in the name of justice, law and order! By legalized process he obtains $1,136 worth of property for which he gave no equivalent whatever. The value of these farms consists solely in the labor expended upon them by D and E and now, through no fault of theirs, but through the fault of the system which they endorsed without understanding, they are forced to surrender to the money loaners their property worth $2,000. He is now able to extort from them rent for values which their own labor has created or drive them and their wives and children out on the highways to tramp, to beg, to steal, perchance to starve and die.

It is pertinent here again to pause and ask the reader to give due reflection to this transaction. Were these men at fault for the loss of their homes and consequent poverty? Had they doubled their labor or quadrupled their economy would it have increased the circulating medium by a single dollar? Most assuredly not, for the number of dollars can only be increased by coinage or importation and only by an actual increase of dollars can these debts be paid.

Returning to the subject of the money loaner's power, it may now be observed that if he forecloses the land in satisfaction of these debt, society will be left in possession of $200; but the banker will by law be permitted to rent these two farms worth $2,000. Interest on money and rents on land usually coincide, and our banker is able to rent these farms on the 10 per cent basis and in one year the rent will bring back to him the ownership of the original $200. This deprives the islanders of all money; and thus deprived, some member or members will be forced again to borrow it on the same terms as did A, B, C and D, and as like causes produce like effects the banker will be able in a few years more to foreclose two or three more homes, thereby giving him still greater power through rent and interest.

Thus year by year the concentration of wealth will increase and homeless men will multiply. By the power these rents and interest give to this money loaner he is able to command the services and products of labor and soon becomes a well-clothed, well-groomed and courteous gentleman. These exterior qualifications always command the respect and admiration of the multitude. His financial success enables him to travel at home and abroad, to appear in the halls of legislation where the people send their representatives; here by the seductive power of his position and the purchasing power of his money he buys their votes and obtains the grant of valuable franchises and the donation of rich lands. These swell his fortune and strengthen his dominion over men. The finality of these transactions will transfer the ownership of the entire island into the hands of this money loaner and leave the original owners serfs and slaves amid the wealth they have by their own labor created.

Returning to COT we find that this $64 of debt impossible of payment has accrued because of a deviation from mathematical law. This deviation cannot be annulled or set aside by statute law. The decree of man can never make the sum of two and two make six; neither can an increase be laid upon our money obligations by legislation without giving the money loaner power to ultimately foreclose the homes of the people, unless said increase is systematically provided for.

The law declaring that 8 per cent or any other is the legal rate of interest is the most infamous power of robbery that ever blackened the pages of a nation's code. Under its exactions and executions the possession of homes soon becomes impossible and hope, happiness, honesty, virtue and patriotism perishes from the hearts of men. Vain will be the display of flags to resuscitate these sentiments.

Like the sinuous trail of the serpent, these dollars move through the channels of trade with such intricacy that their action is unnoticed and unrecorded and their debt-making power is unsuspected. Another factor in the financial system of these islanders may be even more potent than interest in producing debt growth and the concentration of wealth. Referring again to the COT (lending) we will go back to the time when B borrowed the first $100 and paid them to G for wheat. G now owns these $100 and so does A, for A only loaned them to B. To whom do they then belong? And what will become of B's security if G should take them and go to Europe? We will assume that G does not do this, and that he does not need this money for immediate use. He has an eye for business and is willing to turn banker, too, so he loans it to some needy neighbor whom we will call F, who wants it for three years, and who is willing to pay ten percent for its use. The reader will now observe that F's note falls due on the same day that E's and D's falls due, making $394 of debt due with but $200 on the island to meet it.

This deviation from correct or mathematical principles arises from loaning the same dollars twice over making $200 of debt due at the same time, with only $100 to meet it. Neither of these men knew how much money was on the island, nor did they know that any relation existed between the amount of business to be transacted and the amount of money needed; nor did they know that dollars could be made from any other metal than gold.

Fike matters in Hafed's dream, all their transactions were regulated by chance, and so as production increased and population multiplied more and more business was transacted with debt (credit) regardless of the times when these debts fell due or the amount of money they had to meet them, and year by year their failures and foreclosures increased until the island was covered with bonds and mortgages and half the people had lost their homes and property without ever once suspecting the true cause. It is obvious that if debts are made, dollars must be made to cancel them. If more dollars of debt fall due at a given time and place than there are dollars in that place it is evident that the amount of debt above the number of dollars must be either foreclosed, refunded, or repudiated.

Editor's Note:

In some ways, this still makes perfect sense, but in others it doesn't. Because in today's global economy, lots of money gets moved around the world, and the island concept seems so small and limited, nothing like today.

In my opinion, the closest we can come to the concept of this island is to now make the island the world. But if we do that, there's still a problem, because there isn't a finite amount of money. We just print it. There might be a finite amount of oil, that's debated in certain circles. There's almost definitely a finite amount of gold, although we can have no way of knowing how much we could still pull out of the ground or off the various soft beds of water where it can be found.

So the analogy of finite money locked on an island really only works to make a point, therefore one must question if the debt cycle functions the same way, when, in the real world, we do go out and acquire new money. What does that do? It certainly can't allow the downward spiral of debt to function in this same way. But the points are very interesting food for thought.

And we must not forget that what it is now called—Fractional Reserve Banking—is a real thing. And, in my opinion, we're better served to take note of and process what the author lays out here, but not forget about what the real enemy is currently. This vicious style of banking is very much a real thing, and it's the reason that you hear about the entire economy shuttering and quaking at the mere thought of a Bank Run.

A Bank Run means everyone goes to the bank to get their money. Well, that's impossible, because the banks hardly have any money. It's all out on loans and investments with only a few percent left behind, making the bank's rich while the poor people, locked in the proverbial gerbil's wheel running in place, barely even get paid interest on the huge gains made by the banks. On the following page is a picture of the system in place that works much like what the author laid out.

Look to the picture on the next page. In a very basic way, it lays out how it's done. However, I think there's a glaring hole in it that makes the final amount wrong. It doesn't mention what rate money is loaned at or when that gets repaid. Which is one thing this book is really good at showing. Everybody knows loans vary. So, let's say these are 10% one year loans. Digest the picture, and I'll explain afterward what I think the real amount generated looks more like on the following page.

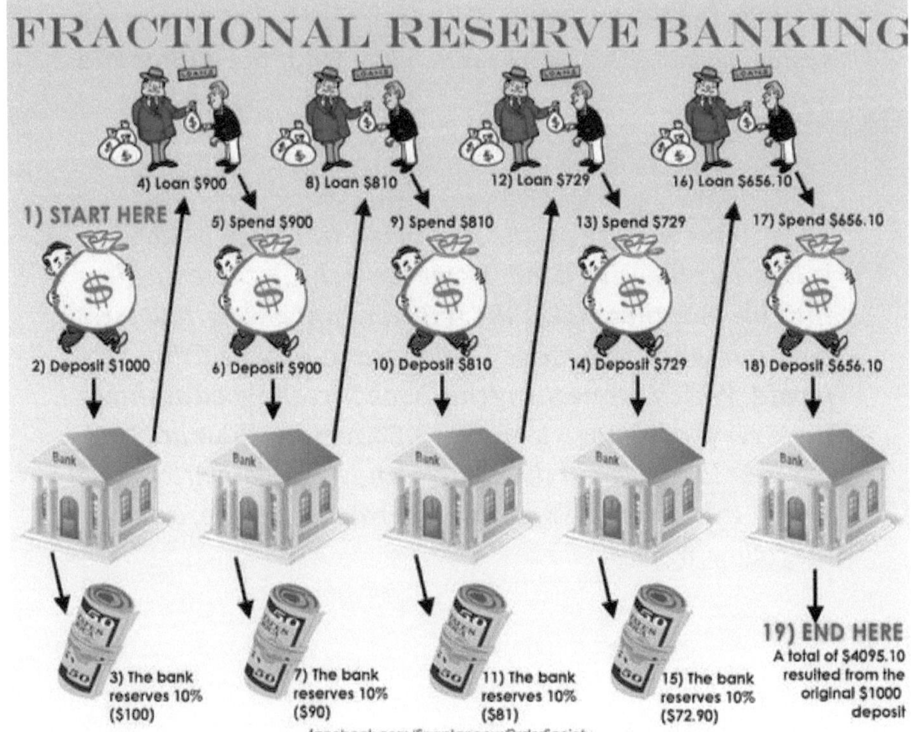

Fractional reserve banking works by retaining only a fraction of what it loans out. This practice expands the money supply, increases risk, and causes inflation. In this example, the initial $1000 deposited expanded to $4095.10. The banks only have $1000, so if everyone went to withdraw their money all at once, there wouldn't be enough to cover all of the obligations. This is known as a

RUN ON THE BANKS

As you can see above, it says loan, but it never says what that loan is. It only leaves the reserve and moves the remainder around. As you probably know, repayment of loans, of course, increases capital. I think the real final result would look something more like this:

Assume a 1 year 10% loan:

-$1,000 deposited & $900 loaned out & $90 in Reserve

-$900 x .1 = $90. 1 year, all repaid = $1,090

To make this simple, since the banks reserve 10% in our example, and the loan is 10%, rather than make a whole table; we can simply double the reserves every bank has in the picture. Look above, $90 is the Reserve, and the 10% loan makes another $90. The picture says all this loaning makes $4,095.10. I submit it doesn't when you factor in that the whole point of this vicious exercise is to make money from loans and plunge the world into, and thereby control it, debt. I submit that with our 10% loan example it makes $4,782.90 after a year, all from an initial $1,000 deposit. In my experience, I've seen banks make far more predatory loans that 10%, haven't you?

Surely if everybody went to the bank to demand their money back, the banks would have no choice but to close their doors and quake in their boots.

CIRCULATION OF CURRENCY

This mathematical deviation exists in the bank-deposit system of the United States, and is at once detected when the banks report four billion dollars on deposit and the Comptroller of the Currency reports less than two billion in circulation, showing four dollars of debt for every dollar in the country. Result: Bank failures, with robbery of the depositors.

The third element which creates debt growth and concentration of wealth, encompassed in the system of exchange, which these islanders endorsed and legalized, is found in the fact that there is not money enough to transact all the business they wish to transact on a cash basis. (Refer to COT) For instance, H has a horse which he desires to sell and J desires to buy. J has no money and no credit at the bank; H, however, believes that J is an honest man, and he is willing to trust him. He sells the horse for $100 and takes J's note for the same, bearing ten percent interest, due in three years. It will now be seen that there are $524 of debt due on the same day, while there are but $200 to meet it. Thus by following these $200 and recording each financial transaction and the date of its maturity, it is found that an increment or growth of $324 of debt has arisen in three years above the amount of dollars to extinguish it. This growth of debt would arise if the number of the same kind of transactions were ten thousand or ten million. This debt growth is the sum of three mathematical deviations from true principle, namely, $124 usury or interest, $100 of debt produced by loaning $100 twice over, and $100 made by buying on credit. There are three ways by which this increment of debt may be extinguished or adjusted. It may be foreclosed, refunded or repudiated.

As all business is run by chance, perhaps all three methods may be used. F may be foreclosed; D may extend his time or refund; J may repudiate by abusing "confidence" and running away to Canada. Or they may pool their wits and succeed in refunding it upon the community by the following method: Let us suppose that D, E, F, and J begin to realize, as they are sure to do, about six months before their debts fall due, that money is very scarce, wages low and work hard to obtain, and from the present outlook they will by no means be able to meet their obligations. They will, if shrewd, begin to cast about to find ways and means of payment. They are good mechanics, and the dilapidated condition of their state house suggests the idea of bonding the island for the purpose of building a new one. They call the people together and convince them of the desirability of the plan. Bonds are issued to the amount of $324. They are sent to London, sold for gold and the money brought into the island. The work begins and D, E, F, and J secure jobs and earn money enough to pay off their individual indebtedness and all the people view with pride and satisfaction the achievement of these industrious men. The banker, too, with smiling suavity, declares with unquestioned authority that, "This is the most prosperous country the sun ever shone upon." But let us take time to reflect. Is the debt of $324 paid, or is it transferred to the collectivity, refunded into a bonded indebtedness against every home on the island ? All understand that bonds are community or collective debts. These bonds have been drawn for twenty years at 5 per cent and at the end of this time the original $324 borrowed from London has been carried back in interest, leaving on the island only $200 with which to pay $324 of bonds.

The principal of these bonds must now be paid by the taxation of the islanders. Every individual must pay his pro rata of taxes. On the island there is but $200. Therefore, some must fail of having the amount necessary to pay taxes with. In the meantime foreign syndicates have located loan agents in every town and hamlet to loan money on farm property, and since by no means can $324 be paid with $200, therefore some among the people, naturally the weakest members of society, made so by sickness or some other unpreventable misfortune, will be obliged to borrow money to meet this taxation to pay off the foreign bonds. Taxation is levied and the bonds are paid and all throw up their caps and shout: "We have paid our debts." The reader will not fail to see that an increment of debt of $124, the difference between $324 and $200, has not been paid. It has again been transferred, this time from the collectivity (all the people of the island) to the individual homes. Another fact of deep significance to these islanders worth the reader's closest attention is that in paying off these foreign bonds these islanders have lost their money volume of $200. The ownership of it has passed over to London. Worse than this; they are individually $124 in debt to these foreign money loaners; and still worse, if they do not at once recognize their right to make or coin money and also understand that a good dollar can be made from any material which they themselves by law decree they will be forever forced to borrow their power of exchange from foreigners, and the growth of debt arising from the usury on these loans will be foreclosed by the foreign money loaners and year by year these islanders will see the ownership of their lands and industries passing into the hands of a foreign country. As long as they maintain the gold standard they will be powerless to stay this foreign absorption. These formulated transactions reveal the methods which produce a growth of debt and the instruments—bonds and mortgages—by which it is perpetuated, being transferred back and forth first from the individual to the collectivity by bonds, then from the collectivity to the individual by taxation. If the mortgages are extinguished the people are bonded collectively; if the bonds are extinguished the people are mortgaged individually. All these processes of bonding, mortgaging, foreclosing, taxing, and renting are going on simultaneously over a wide field of territory among parties unknown to each other. Their record is never kept and their true relation to each other is never comprehended, nor is the increment of debt which arises ever known or provided for, or liquidated except through the foreclosure of securities, which produces the concentration of wealth. These processes continually increase the increment of debt, which grows with their growth and fattens upon their decay until every home on the island is overshadowed with a mortgage and every county, town and city is blanketed with a bond. This increment of debt is impossible of payment unless the amount is known and intelligently provided for by one or all of the three methods which have been previously mentioned.

No amount of industry or frugality on the part of these islanders can abolish this increment of debt or the results which follow it. Even higher, higher rises this floodtide of ruin into thousands, millions, billions; ever faster, faster does it swell the fortunes of the money loaners, until the ownership of their island and its industries passes into the hands of foreign lords and dukes, who send their warships to collect their rents and interest at the point of the bayonet, as has been done in Egypt.

These islanders are now serfs and slaves amidst the wealth their own hands have created, enslaved by endorsing a system of commodity exchange, the philosophy of which they did not understand. For a nation of people doing business by these methods there is absolutely no hope and no salvation; every industry they establish and every home they create must in the end pass into the ownership of the money loaners.

By the use of $200 for three years, on the loans of which 10 per cent increase was legalized in six transactions, none of which were unreasonable or extravagant, it has been possible for a debt of $324 to arise, which is impossible of payment in accordance with the terms of the contract without an increase of money either by coinage or importation. Failing in this, we find $1,736 worth of property foreclosed and concentrated into the hands of a man who never by a single hour's toil honestly earned one penny of it.

The rapidity with which these transactions will accomplish concentration of wealth may be approximately calculated when we find by actual calculation that $200 loaned at 10 per cent and compounded every year will transfer to the money loaner over 65 billion dollars' worth of property, or more than the entire wealth of the United States, in the short period of 184 years.

This is the result when every transaction is legal and characterized with the strictest honesty and integrity; how much more rapidly will the work be consummated when these principles are manipulated by dishonest bankers, capitalists and legislators; when dollars are converted into bonds, when debts are manufactured by law, when the volume of money is expanded and contracted, when millions of it is burned and millions more demonetized, when every juggling trick of fraud and chicanery that the cupidity and greed of man can devise and operate is clearly evidenced by the conditions now existing in the United States, all of which have been produced in the last thirty years! Can human ingenuity devise a more cruel and vicious system of tyranny and spoliation to rob and enslave the people by legally binding them to an impossibility and then compelling them to surrender their property to satisfy this impossibility?

The truth is, the harder these people worked the deeper they sunk in debt and destitution. The more they worked the more they produced; the more they produced the more they had to exchange; the more they had to exchange the more money must be borrowed; the more money borrowed the more the interest accrued; the more interest accrued the faster grew the debt; the larger the debt the more of their earnings were consumed in paying interest, and the more want and destitution they must endure. Enslaved by the power of gold.

To avoid confusion, it has been assumed throughout this illustration that these islanders did not increase their money volume, either by coinage or importation, and that the money loaners did not expend any money during these three years. We will now introduce these factors into our problem by supposing that $50 were coined, $50 were imported and the money loaners expended $24. Then it will be seen that the sum of these will cancel $124 of debt, which will still leave $200 of debt to be foreclosed, refunded or repudiated. By this increase of money the growth of debt and the resulting concentration of wealth will be less rapid, but it will not be extinguished unless the increase of money is equal to the debt growth.

Before leaving this subject to draw conclusions it is worth noting that debts made by loaning the same dollars more than once and debts made by buying on credit may be canceled by the circulation of money when due regard is paid to the time when these debts fall due. For example, suppose B borrows $100 of A and pays a debt he owes C. C loans this to D, who pays his debt to E, who again loans to F. Here is a debt of $300 which has been created by loaning the same $100 three times. If these debts fall due upon the same day we may be reasonably sure that the dollars cannot be made to circulate rapidly enough to cancel these debts; but if the dates are not identical then it will be possible for F to purchase something of B worth $100, who then can pay A. A can buy of D, who can then pay C. He can purchase of F, who then can pay E. These debts have thus all been canceled by circulation. But if B borrows money of A for sixty days and pays his debt to C, who reloans it to B for sixty days, and so on, until it reaches F, who keeps it in his pocket for six months, it will be seen that it is not safe to count on circulation for paying debts, and that the loaning of money over and over again is a dangerous and unscientific method of doing business, which will produce any amount of financial disaster.

Interest, which has been shown to be a factor in creating debt growth, cannot be paid or canceled by the circulation of money when the entire volume is loaned into circulation. It was clearly proved by the first four operations on the chart that interest continually refunded itself, and will always do so unless the coinage, importation of money and the expenditures of the money loaners are equal to the amount of debt accruing by interest. Increase by one or all three of these methods is the only means by which interest can be paid.

We are here confronted by the practical man who says: "Oh, yes, you reformers are all right as theorists, but when it comes to practice your theories do not work. Business is now performed with bank checks and drafts and very little money is needed; in fact, money cuts a very small figure in the business world today. Checks perform all the work." And so he runs on until, out of breath, he is compelled to stop from sheer exhaustion. There is no use in trying to arrest him in his prattle, for he is so badly afflicted with check on the brain that an ounce of fact and philosophy never so carefully administered would prove fatal. The business world has no time today to follow any train of thought to its ultimate conclusion, and so we must endure this sapient prattle until these men personally confront such conditions as will compel them to think and reason.

For the benefit of those who are trying to educate themselves upon this great question we will explain the check system which the bankers are now trying to force the people to believe is so much better than a system of money. A check or draft is an order for the payment of money drawn on a banker and payable at sight.

Before the banker ever issues a check of this character some person must first deposit a sum of money equal to the amount which the check calls for, or money obligations, such as well-secured bonds, iron-clad notes, mortgages, etc., may be sold to the banker at a discount and the proceeds placed to the credit of the seller, against which proceeds he can draw checks. These checks pass from person to person, making exchanges and paying debts. Every person is willing to take the check who believes in the solvency of the bank on which the check is drawn. But no check so issued ever did or could perform any more exchanges or cancel any more debts than the dollars which were deposited to obtain it. And if these dollars had been used instead of the check just as much business would have been performed. In the course of business transactions these checks must finally come into the possession of persons who will present them to the bank on which they were drawn to be redeemed in money, or they may, if drawn on different banks, be canceled at the clearing house. For instance H deposits $100 in bank No. 1 and receives a check. J deposits $100 in bank No. 2 and receives a check also. These checks may perform hundreds of exchanges and cancellations of debts and finally be canceled themselves at the clearing house, if it should happen that check No. 1 should fall into the possession of bank No. 2 and check No. 2 should come into the ownership of bank No. 1.

But still no more business has been done or exchanges performed than could have been performed with the money on which the check was issued. When bonds, notes, mortgages, and other debt obligations are discounted by the banker and checks issued to the sellers these checks, too, will make exchanges and cancel debts the same as checks drawn on actual cash. These checks may also cancel themselves at the clearing house, but when so canceled this does not cancel the notes, bonds and mortgages held by the banker nor prevent the banker from demanding settlement, in money, of those persons who drew and signed these evidences of debt. And as these were drawn for the want of sufficient quantity of circulating medium no increase of business was secured by them above that which would have been performed by creating dollars instead of debts. No substitute for the dollar can ever perform more work than the dollar itself. The check can transact no more business than the dollars which were deposited to secure the check, neither can they avert the payment of debts nor prevent more dollars of debt accruing than there are dollars to meet these debts nor the results of foreclosure and failure which follow.

Let the reader carefully note that it is not the dollar, nor any legitimate action of the dollar, which produces financial disturbances, but it is debt contracts (bonds, mortgages and notes) which follow the loan of the dollar that create failures, foreclosures and panics. So long as the dollar performs its legitimate function in exchanging production from person to person no evil effect follows its use. Every debt is an evidence of the insufficiency and inadequacy of the power or medium of exchange.

The remedy for the evils from which we suffer will be found in making dollars instead of debts.

To see a whole nation full of people wildly, madly rushing hither and thither, from pillar to post, from Maine to Alaska, Florida to California from city to city, from state to state and from one nation to another crossing oceans, scaling mountains, facing arctic frosts and tropic fevers, searching, struggling, scheming schemes that mortal never dared to scheme before; even schemes of robbery and murder against their brother-man, all to get dollars, at the same time persistently, stubbornly, idiotically, denying themselves the right to coin them, is a sad commentary on the intelligence of the nineteenth century.

We have now logically, scientifically and mathematically demonstrated beyond the possibility of doubt or disputation the impossibilities imbedded in a system of commodity exchange where the commodity is insufficient in volume to do business on a cash basis and where it is loaned into circulation with an increase attached to the loan. It scarcely need be suggested that if the size of the island, the number of the people and the money of the bank were doubled, or if two banks were established, each with $200 capital, the growth of debt and the power of wealth concentration would be doubled also.

If all these factors were multiplied by ten no change in the relations of debt and absorption would occur. Or if the banks were ten thousand, their loaning capital $2,000,000,000 instead of $200, and the number of people seventy million, there would be no material change in the mathematical relations and results. Debt growth and the concentration of wealth are the natural and mathematical results that will always follow these methods of doing business.

The only reason we are unable to calculate the precise time when bankruptcy will occur is because we do not keep the record of every transaction which produces an unpayable debt and all the factors which extinguish or liquidate it. Money is a species of bookkeeping with a debit and credit side which must be correctly kept and balanced.

It is in season now to ask the reader specifically to designate the differences, if any, between the methods employed by these islanders for securing a medium of exchange and the methods employed and legalized by the people of the United States. It is here affirmed that they are one and the same; identical in processes;

identical in results; differing only in the volume of money used, the number of people using it and the size of the territory occupied by the system.

To prove otherwise it would be necessary to know how many dollars of debt arise from interest, how many from loaning the same dollars more than once and how many are made by buying on credit and the identical dates on which all these debts fall due. It would also be necessary to know how many dollars are coined, how many are exported from the country, how many are imported into the country, how many are taken out of circulation, how many are lost and the exact amount of the expenditures of the money loaners. Failing to know all these items, our gold standard opponents are at sea in a tub, neither having chart, compass, pilot nor rudder; no, not even the guiding ray of the polar star. They see not the whirlpool just ahead that will swamp their craft and immerse them in the same waters of financial ruin in which many so many of their fellow citizens have been submerged.

By these illustrations all the factors of our financial system have been examined and traced. Summing up, we find three factors or elements which produce debt growth—viz., interest, loaning the same dollars more than once and buying on credit. There are three ways by which this debt growth might be liquidated without loss or foreclosure—viz., by coinage, by importing money from foreign countries, (by exporting more goods than are imported and by the expenditures of travelers) and by the expenditures of the creditor classes. If the sum total of these three does not equal the debt growth there are three ways by which it is adjusted. It may be foreclosed, repudiated or refunded. All three of these methods of adjustment are employed, dealing great injustice and wrong to all the parties concerned. If debts are foreclosed the creditor usually secures about three times the value he loaned, which is a cruel injustice to the debtor, by taking something for which no equivalent bas been given. If debts are repudiated then the creditor loses that which rightfully belongs to him and he is the injured party.

If debts are refunded the evil day when one or the other of these alternatives must occur is deferred. No record of these three items of debt increase is ever kept, nor is their sum total ever known, and no provision for the honest extinguishment of debt growth is ever made. So year by year the concentration of wealth increases by our failures and foreclosures, and year by year our debts enlarge by being refunded and the interest compounded.

There is no practical way of providing for this increase of debt under the present system unless the number of dollars is increased to the extent of the debt growth; failing in this it constantly refunds itself, and as our money becomes more difficult to obtain because the securities which must be put up in order to obtain money constantly diminish, until finally they all become covered with bonds and mortgages and money almost wholly disappears from circulation. Chaos follows. It will also be apparent that if an amount of money equal to the debt growth was obtained and thrown into circulation without debt very few, if any, failures would occur. So vast have been the exploitations of the people of the United States by and through these processes that one stands appalled not only at the magnitude of the crime but at the stupidity or treachery of the economists and statesmen in their failure to expose it. Debt upon debt; foreclosure upon foreclosure; panic upon panic; disaster upon disaster, until we, a robbed and robbing people, stand upon the very brink of national bankruptcy and disruption.

These processes have been going on so long, and these intricate relations here described are so little understood that those who are benefited by them have come to look upon them as honest and legitimate, and those who have been the victims have become accustomed to regard their misfortunes as the results of their own mismanagement or the allotments of an inscrutable Providence, whose decrees it were impious to question. For thirty years a greedy set of grasping cormorants and inhuman vultures, whose principal dens of devastation are located in London and Wall street, have by these processes, and others still more infamous, pillaged the people and confiscated the land until a wail of despair ascends from millions of crushed and bleeding hearts and the nation is filled with homeless, penniless multitudes who unable even to obtain employment.

That these demonstrations give true interpretation to the causes which have led to our deplorable condition of congested wealth and unpayable debt of $40,000,000,000 must be so glaringly apparent that the wayfaring man, though a gold-standard Republican, may not be fooled again.

For thirty years the American people have been admonished by one of the most impressive and suggestive object lessons ever enacted before the eyes of intelligent men without once arousing their suspicion or enlisting their serious consideration. For a quarter of a century Bradstreet and Dun have reported through the weekly and daily papers "219 failures this week, against 217 of the corresponding week of last year;" "225 failures this week against 219 of the corresponding week of last year," and so on until 425 failures were reported in a single week (July, 1893). Week in and week out, month in and month out, year in and year out, this red flag of anarchy has been flung in their faces without their comprehending its awful meaning or putting forth any adequate effort to investigate the causes which have led to these widespread disasters. When questioned their only reply is: "It always was and it always will be," or "People fail because they do not have sense enough to run a business." There is a grim truth in this last remark which is truly pathetic. Interest is in every sense unjust and unscientific and the nation that travels over a highway paved with bonds, iron-clad notes and cutthroat debt obligations travels the road of legalized robbery and financial ruin, at the end of which lies the precipice of anarchy and national dissolution. The dumb inarticulate cry of "interest, interest," now heard throughout the length and breadth of the land is but the roar of the surging breakers just ahead toward which our beloved country—the greatest and grandest Republic ever organized—is blindly, madly rushing with ever-increasing impetuosity.

From that point of time buried so far away in the catacombs of the dead past that all memory of it has been obliterated from the archives of history, when the prehistoric nations made gold and silver their medium and power of exchange, the curse of debt impossible of payment has eaten up the substance of the people and destroyed the stability of all forms of government. At first a small cloud, no larger than a man's hand, at last a hideous, whirling cyclone, black with crime and freighted with destruction. And thus it always must be with all nations to the end of all time who use gold and silver for their power and medium of exchange. Like causes will produce like effects.

Historical evidence is not wanting, both ancient and modern, to confirm these conclusions. So well did Moses, the great lawgiver of the Jewish people, comprehend the disaster of debt which lay imbedded in commodity exchange that he wisely instituted laws which, if they had been observed, would have counteracted both the concentration of wealth, and the growth of debt.

Editor's Note:

> *I find this part very interesting, considering there's no way the author could have foreseen modern technology, and the*

new modern currency created, we think, by regular people —Crypto Currency—and of course the big dog, Bitcoin. People, even if they've never read anything like this book, intrinsically know that this slave-making banking system we currently have has them bent over a rail. And having our own currency system that we run through each other, bypassing the banks, scares the hell out of them. That's why they're doing everything in their power, in my opinion, to gain control of Crypto Currency, and then either crush it, or just adopt it and make it the new debt instrument that further enslaves humanity. It wouldn't matter at that point what they decided to do with it.

This is why everybody should own bitcoin and others, and people should go ahead and just make their own economies. Yes, many, many economies, too many for governments to count. It has been tried on the Dark Web, is currently still being tried, and you can bet everything you have that any government will do what it can to suppress it, control it, and eliminate it. Or else, there might be people they don't truly have control over, the horror.

People should be connecting and buying and selling with Crypto right now. It would be disorganized at first, but we have social media, and we have a currency they can't really control. My god, people slap things up for sale on Facebook and meet in parking lots to make a transfer, and the government has almost no control over it, because it would be too difficult. Are you telling me we can't add crypto to the equation? There's just NO WAY! It's impossible. Really? We can fly in planes and take rockets to space, but find a way through social media to create an economy powered by Crypto? That's impossible. [Insert meme here:] Sure, Jan.

THE MONEY PROBLEM

A friendly critic pronounces this last sentence unscientific and requests that it be stricken out. This critic may never have come to regard money as a tool or instrument by the means of which a certain kind of work is to be performed. When he does he will see that it is as unscientific, and consequently uneconomical, to manufacture money from a material more expensive than utility demands as it would be to make any other tool, or instrument from a material more expensive than is demanded by its use. If all the governments of the world should assume the ownership of all the gold and silver and also all the mines now known to exist and give to gold and silver money exclusively the legal tender quality, there would not be a sufficient quantity to do the business of the world on a cash basis; and debts arising from doing business on credit would increase the same as the debts which arise from interest and would be unpayable only through foreclosure. Therefore we must conclude that both gold and silver are unscientific material on which to place the money stamp. Our problem rests not only with the material from which money is made, but also with methods of circulation and the liquidation of debt. All debts must be made possible of payment by an adequate circulation scientifically disbursed.

The law which absolutely forbade usury prevented the growth of that part of debt which is unpayable without an increase of money. The law repudiating all debts every seven years prevented the growth of that part of debt which arises from buying on credit and the re-loaning of the same money more than once. Then to prevent the concentration of wealth, which arose through the foreclosure of debts during the six years in which there was no releasement; the fiftieth year was proclaimed the year of Jubilee: when all the lands that had passed out of the hands of the debtor class were restored back to the original possessors.

The power of metallic money or commodity exchange to create debt impossible of payment and the concentration of wealth which would follow was most surely known to Moses, else these counteracting laws, which on the surface have the most decided appearance of injustice, would not have been instituted in the Jewish code and the direct curses of God pronounced against the people if they disregarded them. Obedience to these laws would have so preserved equality of wealth and opportunities that the prophets of a later day would not have bewailed the pitiful conditions of Judea, saying, "Our inheritance is turned to strangers, our houses to aliens." (Lament 5:2); "the young children ask bread, and no man breaketh it unto them." (Lament 4:4); "The hands of the pitiful women have sodden their own children" (Lament 4:10); "Our skin was black like an oven because of the terrible famine." (Lament 5:10). This wisdom of the ancients seems always to have been the inheritance of the Jews, and while they have no country and scattered among many nationalities, where often they are not permitted to own land, yet so well do they understand the power of money when loaned that seldom ever see a Jew who is either a tramp or a pauper. Acting upon this ancient knowledge, the House of Rothschilds, with a few co-religionists, conspire to own the world.

Exodus 22, 25; Deut 15, 25, 28; Ezekiel 18; Nehemiah 5. The power to accomplish their design will be readily understood by a few mathematical calculations. The National bonds drawn upon the various nations of the earth are now estimated to be 28 billion, largely, if not wholly, held in London. This is three and one half times all metallic money of the world, which reveals the fact that the money of the world is primarily owned in London and the nations of the earth are doing business with borrowed money, owning not one dollar of their circulating medium. These bonds are drawing 4% interest, which annually amounts to $1,120,000,000. This is more than three times the annual output of all the gold and silver in the world, and seven and one-half times the output of the world's gold.

The world's interest-bearing debts are now estimated to be a over 200 billion dollars, which is twenty-five times all the gold and silver money in the world and fifty times the amount of the world's gold. The annual interest at 10 percent would be 20 billion dollars, which is a sum fifty-four times greater than the world's annual output of both gold and silver and 108 times the world's annual output of gold.

The power of this vast growth of debt to concentrate the ownership of the world into the hands of the few men who own the gold must certainly be comprehended by all who will study these calculations, and the man who cannot understand that this work will be accomplished in one-half the time when silver is demonetized is too imbecile to be allowed the privilege of voting. All this vast debt has accrued by three mathematical deviations which have been described—namely, interest, loaning the same dollars more than once, and buying on credit. There is but one cure. Dollars must be made instead of bonds, notes and mortgages.

The last pages of this book will clearly demonstrate the success of the money mongers. What a marvelous contrast between the laws for the protection of the debtor classes, as established by Moses, and the Roman law, 11 of the twelve tables, which sanctioned the creditor, after some preliminary formalities, to scourge a debtor to death, and if the debtor had several creditors they might cut his body in pieces, each taking a piece in proportion to the amount of his debt. If the creditors did not resort to this horrible atrocity they were authorized to reduce him to slavery and subject him to chains and stripes or sell him and his wife and children into foreign slavery. The laws of Greece prior to Solon were little less severe than those of ancient Rome, except the creditor was not permitted to kill his debtor. The cultivating tenants and small farmers weighed down by debt were first deprived of their property and finally with their families were reduced to slavery. The growth of debt went on until all the small farmers and were converted into slaves and there grew up but two classes in the state—the large land owners and the poor debtors reduced to slavery.

Editor's Note:

As I've touched on already, I don't think this money point the author makes is irrelevant, and I understand doing things just for an example, but in today's global economy and global tourism, money literally flows around the world, and it literally gets printed all the time.

It's hard to imagine a situation more different from what the author pitches to make the debt example. Nowadays, I think that people are more debt slaves, because of high interest rates and using credit all the time, rather than because new money isn't injected to almost all places all the time. It is. But you bury people in debt, and guess what? They're buried in debt. It doesn't matter how well money flows around the world. There's just so much debt.

Ironically, as I was talking about Crypto Currency in my

last note, I was reviewing this section, and I realized, you know what does have finite amounts available? Lots of Crypto does. Some, mostly worthless , currencies make the maximum number of coin something in the billions. And other, mostly valuable, currencies limit the number somewhere in the multiple millions like Bitcoin, not hundreds of millions.

I'm good enough with investments to know that limiting the number makes it more valuable, but it's much more abstract for me to imagine that limited number of coins with debt attached. I guess it would look a lot like what is laid out in this book with the money finite and locked on an island and A, B, C, D, and so on, moving it around while the lender attaches interest to it and gradually ends up with everything. We can't let that happen.

I'll reiterate what I said in the previous note about a real, proper, Crypto economy. We must make it and make it official, and it must be only buying and selling, and/or trading. The moment a lender gets his greasy foot in the door, it's all over. The cycle of interest sucks up everything, especially when you actually have a finite number of coins like Crypto does.

It's a train wreck just waiting to happen, and it probably already does, and I just haven't found out yet that it's really a thing. Well, if it is a thing, people should be responsible to do whatever is in their power to un-make it a thing. It's that big of a deal.

SPEECH OF JUDGE HENRY C. CALDWELL.

Between the arrogant profligacy of the rich and the destitution and misery of the slaves the state was about to perish. In its extremity it was saved by the justice and the wisdom of Solon. He abolished imprisonment for debt; set all slaves free who had been adjudged so for debt and canceled all contracts in which the debtor had borrowed on the security of his person or his land. Mortgage debts were repudiated by pulling down the stone pillars erected on the land which were at that time used to record the debt.

Coming down to recent events, our own history affords a striking example corroborative of the position here elucidated. During the war nearly $2,000,000,000 were thrown into circulation without debt. The result was, to an extent never before known, the debtor classes were able and did pay their debts and the failures of the country were reduced to a minimum, being respectively 485, 502, 530, and 532 for the four years 1863, 1864, 1865, and 1866! Then came the contraction policy with all its withering, blighting curse of sheriffs' sales, mortgage foreclosures and business failure—2,386 of them in 1867! Since this time there has been a steady increase, until now they have reached nearly 16,000 in a single year and our growth of debt is over $2,000,000,000 a year, or over six million every twenty-four hours. This appaling phenomena can be accounted for upon no other hypothesis than that laid down here. Let him who thinks it can be, at once proceed to enlighten this distracted world that these appalling losses which send men down to poverty and crime may soon be numbered with the things of the past. From this analysis which encompasses and shows the relation of every factor in our financial system and agrees with all known facts we must conclude that business done with borrowed money on which interest accrues and by buying on credit must always result disastrously unless the coinage equals the debt growth or it is otherwise provided for.

If the reader still doubts, let him carefully study the following table and note the decrease and increase of failures, with the increase and decrease of coinage. By the use of $200 for three years, on the loans of which 10 per cent increase was legalized, in six transactions, none of which were based upon unreasonable or improbable conditions, it has been proved that it was possible for a debt of $324 to accumulate which was impossible of payment in accordance with the terms of the contract without an increase of money either by coinage or importation. Failing in this we find $1,736 worth of property concentrated into the hands of a man who never by a single hour's toil honestly earned one penny of it.

In the United States we find ten or twelve thousand banks and loan associations loaning into circulation a sum of money varying from one to two billion dollars, which is the entire volume, by the same methods and similar terms. By the bank-deposit system we find this same volume of money loaned over and over again, probably not less than four times. Thousands of pawnshops and private individuals are loaning money on rates of interest varying from ten to three hundred per cent. Thousands and tens of thousands of transactions are effected by means of promissory notes and promises to pay. The increase of our money volume is not one-thousandth part of the debt growth, while, as will be seen by the table on page 44, many years show a positive decrease. We see the same results of business failures, foreclosures, panics, concentration of wealth and debt growth, as was seen on the island. By these financial methods the people of the United States, who are the most energetic, inventive and industrious on earth, have, while working to their utmost, imposed upon themselves a debt of $40,000,000,000 in the last thirty years; while not less than about the same amount has either been repudiated or foreclosed. The preceding table only partially reveals the magnitude of these crimes, for in this table neither the failures below three thousand nor the foreclosure of real estate are recorded.

Let no one who reads this blackest page of human history ever again raise his voice against these destitute, homeless multitudes, contemptuously asserting that "it is their own fault; they have brought these evils upon themselves by their own extravagance and idleness." It is infamously false. By the legalized processes here described, nine-tenths of these afflicted and stricken people have been robbed of their homes, their labors, and their education. What if in their ignorance and poverty they do not understand the methods employed to rob them? An avenging eye beholds it all and the oppressor shall not pass out from under the rod until he has paid the utmost farthing. Your gains have been filched from the poor; from you these riches shall melt as snow before the summer's sun. From these deductions there is no escape; that which ye sow ye shall reap. Your gold and silver is cankered and the rust of them shall eat your soul as with fire. [James 5:3]

My task is done. This chart, sublime in its simplicity, proclaims to a world lying in darkness the scientific solution of that so long unsolved problem of which Blanqui exclaimed: "Happy our generation if science sometime gives the key." It reveals the incantations and machinations complained of by Senator Ingalls, by which one-half the wealth of this great nation has been legally stolen from the hands of those who created it, and the ownership of it transferred to those who gave no equivalent for it—the idle few. Hitherto the only epitaph man has inscribed over the buried achievements of his past greatness is "Nations rise, and nations fall." But henceforth this chart shall point with unerring certainty to the disease—concentration of wealth—and the cause of this is debt produced by the use of gold and silver money. Go forth; thy mission is as broad as humanity; thy power as great as truth.

AFTERWORD

In closing, I hope readers find this book as interesting as it was for me to edit it and write in it. I also hope that people gain, if they don't already have it, an understanding of why Crypto Currency is so important, and why it's so equally important to not let it become a tool to create debt. If it was the only currency we had left, the world would be eventually consumed by it and enslaved to debt, trying to trudge pointlessly through mucky swamps of interest only to run into jagged mountains of debt.

Debt, is something we must eliminate from this world, and there's no way to eliminate it by force. The powers are too great that hold it locked in place. The only way is for people to free themselves of those shackles. If you put yourself in debt, you must carry yourself and the chains it puts you in.

Only people, a people, who rid themselves of debt can destroy it, and I fear that this too may be impossible. The Debtors know this. They know that they only need to dangle something shiny in front of some people and offer it on credit. It's too easy. If there's any hope left for humanity, maybe these people can learn to stop.

We'll see...

www.ingramcontent.com/pod-product-compliance
Ingram Content Group UK Ltd.
Pitfield, Milton Keynes, MK11 3LW, UK
UKHW041849190726
13854UKWH00002B/800

9 798630 335401